HOW TO BECOME THE BEST

Caregiver

TAKE CARE OF YOURSELF
DURING THIS PROCESS READ MY BOOK
AND I WILL SHOW YOU HOW!

EARLENE MCCUTCHEN-ATIBA

 ARCHWAY
PUBLISHING

Archway Publishing books may be ordered through booksellers or by contacting:

Archway Publishing
1663 Liberty Drive
Bloomington, IN 47403
www.archwaypublishing.com
844-669-3957

ISBN: 978-1-4808-8634-6 (sc)
ISBN: 978-1-4808-8635-3 (e)

Library of Congress Control Number: 2019920761

Print information available on the last page.

Archway Publishing rev. date: 08/28/2021

The faith and confidence of others in me have been like shining, guiding stars.

—Marian Anderson

The two most important days of your life are the day you were born and the day you find out why.

—Mark Twain

On Taking Time for Ourselves:

Each person deserves a day away in which no problems are confronted, no solutions searched for. Each of us needs to withdraw from the cares which will not withdraw from us. A day away acts as a spring tonic. It can dispel rancor, transform indecision, and renew the spirit.

—Maya Angelou

This book is dedicated to my wonderful late parents, Leroy and Daisy McCutchen, who taught me about caring, sharing, and having compassion.

To all my wonderful relatives and friends who have supported my efforts during this process, I appreciate the lessons I've learned from you. Thank you for your unconditional support and everlasting love.

CONTENTS

Part 1: Caregiver

Part 2: Taking Care of Yourself

My Mission

To provide valuable information on how to become the best caregiver. To show you how to take care of yourself during the time you are a caregiver.

My Vision

To produce a book that will help all who are caregivers or future caregivers.

My Core Values

To learn something new every day and to share that information with others.

PREFACE

I began my journey as a caregiver at the age of nineteen. This was during the 1970s, when the term *caregiver* was not utilized. The method of caregiving before the 1970s was termed as caring for a loved one. This process involved taking a person into your home to care for him or her. It was considered a family's responsibility to care for a person who could no longer care for himself or herself. Now we have nursing homes and assisted living facilities to care for those who are seniors or are disabled and no longer have the ability to care for themselves. We now live in a society where we leave the responsibility of caring for our loved ones to institutions.

My father was diagnosed with colon cancer in 1969, when he was in the final stages. My father's doctor decided the best course of action would be to resection my father's colon and provide him with a colostomy bag. The process of caring for my father was a family effort. The entire family had to become educated about his type of cancer. The training that the hospital provided encompassed everything from diet, to dispensing medication, to changing his colostomy bag.

I worked for a small insurance company located within walking distance of our home. Working so close to home allowed me to come home during my lunch break. I would change my father's colostomy bag, administer his medication, and prepare his lunch. My mother would sometimes administer his medication, and she'd help bathe him in the mornings and evenings. My sister would help with his evening meals. This routine was carried out until his passing in 1970.

I became my mother's caregiver in 2001. I relocated to Savannah, Georgia, in 1998, coming from Philadelphia, Pennsylvania. My mother continued to live in Philadelphia. In 1999, she developed a very bad bedsore. The cavity was four inches deep and six inches wide. This required her to have a feeding tube placed in her stomach. This was the only way for the bedsore to heal, from the inside out.

After a short stay in the hospital, it came time for my mother to be discharged. I was informed by the hospital that my mother had to be placed in a nursing home. After receiving this information, I needed to locate a nursing home in Savannah that would provide twenty-four-hour care. I could not monitor my mother's care in Philadelphia, Pennsylvania, while I resided in Savannah. I found a nursing home in Savannah that provided the services I needed.

My mother was transported to Savannah on September 1999 aboard a medevac. A registered nurse and a doctor were also on board. I was my mother's caregiver until her passing in 2002. During the process of caring for my mother, I took the responsibility of caring for my brother, who was mentally challenged, for whom my mother had been providing care until her illness. I cared for my brother until his sudden passing in 2005.

"At that point, I became my husband's caregiver"? His left leg was amputated to the hip in 2004 because of an accident. In 2011, he began in-center dialysis treatments. In 2012 we began home hemodialysis treatments. I went through extensive training to become a home dialysis technician. This training was provided by Fresenius Medical Care in Savannah. Their home dialysis department provided me with the training I needed. The center has a small staff of nurses who do an awesome job. They are wonderful, supportive, and caring, providing twenty-four-hour access. They assist with any questions or concerns about the medical aspect of providing dialysis treatments at home. These wonderful team of professionals were available to help me by answering my questions and addressing my concerns. They also assisted with any crisis that I encountered. One word to describe this dynamic team of nurses is *awesome*! The wonderful tech support team also was available 24/7 if I had questions or concerns about the dialysis equipment.

As you read *How to Become the Best Caregiver*, you will find that I've had a great deal of experience with being a caregiver, having dealt with many different situations over the years. My reason for writing *How to Become the Best Caregiver* is to share my experiences with those who are caregivers, with those who may become caregivers in the future, and with those who may be struggling as caregivers. I want to share with you what I've learned as a caregiver on this day-to-day journey. And, trust me, it is a day-to-day journey. This journey will be both challenging and rewarding.

When you get to the end of *How to Become the Best Caregiver*, you will be more informed, you will be more aware, you will have more understanding, you will be more knowledgeable, and you will have become more caring, giving, loving, kind, and considerate of others who are in need of a caregiver. The idea of becoming a caregiver is something you should not entertain lightly. It is an awesome responsibility for those who are up for the challenge. *How to Become the Best Caregiver* will inspire you to become the best caregiver ever. It will give you the tools you need to do so. Utilize *How to Become the Best Caregiver* as both a reference tool and a source of inspiration. It will help you remain focused on the task at hand so you will become the best caregiver you can be. During this process, you will also learn how to take care of yourself. One cannot become, and remain, a healthy, effective, and efficient caregiver if one does not take care of oneself as well.

INTRODUCTION

This is a must-read book. Like no other; it will help you to become the best caregiver ever. This is not just a book. This is a step-by-step guide to help you through the process of becoming the best caregiver possible. *How to Become the Best Caregiver* will help you to develop organizational skills. This will help you stay focused and healthy. *How to Become the Best Caregiver* will make you an expert in documentation. You will also learn time management. This is a very important component. *How to Become the Best Caregiver* will also help you to properly take care of yourself and the person you are caring for. You will learn how to utilize the information herein in such a manner that it lasts you a lifetime. The information in *How to Become the Best Caregiver* focuses on three main components of caregiving that I have experienced. Read the information, absorb the information, and act upon the information. Follow the process that I have outlined in *How to Become the Best Caregiver*, and the result will show that you have become the best and the healthiest caregiver ever. Through caregiving, I found out why I was born. Find out if it is why you were born too.

ACKNOWLEDGMENTS

I would like to acknowledge and give special thanks to the wonderful team of health care professionals who cared for my husband, Muata, over the past seven years: Hope Burnsed, RN (in-center manager—Muata's in-center dialysis nurse); Donna Lombardo, RN (Muata's first home dialysis manager), who trained me to become the best home hemodialysis technician I could be; Crystal Miller, RN (Muata's second home dialysis manager); Lauren L. Chapman, RN (kidney care advocate); Dr. Edward J. Cohn Jr. (vascular surgeon); Dr. Eric Bernstein (nephrologist); Dr. Mark Manocha (optometrist); Dr. Lillian Williams (podiatrist); Dr. Lawrence Zottoli (primary care physician); and Jim Chaplin, director of floor operations for Abilities Unlimited and Hospice Savannah. I thank all the wonderful and thoughtful health care professionals and other professionals who went above and beyond in the care they provided for my husband. They provided him with the best of care and were of enormous support for me. Words are not enough to express my deep gratitude to you all.

Part I
CAREGIVER

What is a caregiver? A caregiver is a person who gives care to someone who does not have the ability to care for himself or herself. A caregiver is a special person willing to take on the awesome responsibility of caring for someone else. A caregiver is one who makes sacrifices. A caregiver is one who is patient, loving, understanding, and caring. A caregiver must not allow himself or herself to become a crutch. A caregiver must be caring and supportive for the people who are in his or her care. A caregiver must be firm yet gentle. A caregiver must be compassionate and show compassion. The caregiver advocates for the people for whom he or she cares, being the voice of one who is unable to speak, the eyes of one whose vision has become hazy, and the ears of one who is unable to hear. Caregivers become protectors, keeping those cared for safe.

As a caregiver, you must be organized and efficient and have an eye for detail. A caregiver must be honest in all areas; however, there are some exceptions. Let me give you an example: My mother suffered from a mild case of dementia. At times, she would ask about certain family members and friends, wondering if they had passed away or were sick. I would not tell her. After caring for my mother for a period of time, I came to the realization that unpleasant information would not benefit her and would only aggravate her mental state, possibly cause her to worry and become irritated. So I made the decision not to give her any negative or sad news at any time. When you are caring for someone whose mental state is like my mother's, it's best to always give good news.

The following things are vital to being a good caregiver:

- Dependability
  The person for whom you care depends upon you for everything and expects you to give the best care possible, regardless of what you may be experiencing.

- Reliability

  The caregiver is relied upon to supply all the needs of the person for whom he or she provides care.

- Compassion

  Showing compassion is not a sign of weakness on your part as a caregiver, but is a demonstration of caring, understanding, and strength regarding the situation of the one for whom you provide care.

- Love

  Always demonstrate sincere love. The person being cared for can tell when you don't.

- Taking care of yourself

  As a caregiver, you must take care of yourself in order to take care of someone else. Caring for yourself reassures the person you care for that you have the knowledge and ability to care for him or her.

- Having a pleasant personality

  A pleasant personality should shine through at all times in a caregiver. To achieve success and excellence as a caregiver, you must demonstrate and show pleasantness.

CHAPTER 1

Before Becoming a Caregiver

There are more than seventy million baby boomers in the United States. The 2010 US Census recorded the greatest number, and the greatest proportion, of people age sixty-five and older in all decennial census history: 40.3 million, or 13 percent of the total population. This boomer generation effect will continue for decades. These numbers may not reflect the handicapped, children, or those with mental or emotional problems who need caregivers.

If you have a mother, a father, another family member, or a friend who may be in need of a caregiver, the first thing you must do is observe and document everything taking place with that person, along with details about his or her living conditions. Make absolutely sure the person is in need of a caregiver, and make absolutely sure you are up for the responsibility and challenge of becoming a caregiver. As a caregiver, you must be organized, you must be focused, and you must have a daily routine to follow. Spend about three days—overnight if you can—with the person to complete this observation. Taking this assessment will help you to determine if a caregiver is warranted and if the person in question wants to have a caregiver. The reason for asking if the person agrees to have a caregiver is that some people who need a caregiver assume they will lose their independence as a person. This is the time to reinforce your responsibility as a caregiver. One of those responsibilities is not to take away the independence of the one being cared for. Rather, you are there to help that person keep his or her independence. If he or she is comfortable with the facts you have presented, then, and only then, should you go forward with the process described in *How to Become the Best Caregiver.*

As I've already stated, the first task is to observe the person's actions and to ask some questions when necessary. This observation will help to establish not only the physical state, but also the mental and emotional states, of the person in question. Following is a list of observations, questions, and checks and balances. When you ask a question regarding a particular issue, listen to the response, and also to what is not being said. Here's an example:

> "When was the last time you had water?"
> "I drink a lot of juice, which has water in it."

This response lets you know that the person may not be drinking enough water.

Eating

Observe the eating habits of the person to whom you provide care. What types of foods is he or she eating. Is he or she eating too much? Not enough? Does he or she eat a lot of junk food or processed foods? Does the person have the ability to cook for him or herself? Does he or she follow a special diet or have a menu? Does the person have the ability to go food shopping?

Sleeping

Observe sleeping and resting habits. Is the person getting enough sleep? Is he or she resting during sleeping time? Ask the questions "Are you getting too much sleep?"; "Can you sleep at all?"; "Are you taking a sleeping aid to help you sleep?"; "If so, is it prescription or over-the-counter?"

Mobility

Is the person mobile? Is he or she able to go to the bathroom on his or her own, or does he or she need assistance? Is the person in a wheelchair? If so, is it a mobility wheelchair or a manual wheelchair? Does he or she need assistance walking with a walker or a cane?

Fluid Intake

How much water is the person drinking during the course of a day? What other liquids is he or she drinking during the day, and how much? Ask the questions.

Medications, Supplements, and Vitamins

If the person is taking prescription medication, observe whether he or she is taking the medication on time, at the correct dosage, and with the correct frequency. If on prescription medication, the person may be on a restricted diet. Also check for any supplements he or she may be taking. Check for dosage, frequency, and the purpose for taking the supplements. Usually supplements are taken because the body may not be producing enough minerals or vitamins. This can occur when someone gets older, has a special type of illness, or is taking a certain type of prescription medication.

Personal Hygiene

Observe personal and oral hygiene. Is the person bathing? Is he or she brushing his or her teeth or cleaning dentures on a daily basis? Make sure underclothing is changed daily; ask the question if necessary. Check the hamper for clothing that needs laundering. This will give you a clear picture of daily personal hygiene, which is important for a person's physical, mental, and emotional well-being.

Living Conditions

Observe all living, cooking, sleeping, and bathing areas for cleanliness, bugs, and rodent infestation. There is a widespread occurrence of bedbug infestation in this country. The efforts to eradicate bedbugs continue. Bedbug bites do not cause diseases in people, but they can lead to inflammation and possible secondary infection from excessive scratching.

Bedbugs

Here are the top four ways to find out whether bedbugs are nearby:

1) Check indoor cracks and crevices under low-light conditions.
2) Look for small blood drops in the home (wet or dry) or brown spots (fecal matter). After engorging, bedbugs may excrete part of their meal, which leaves visible stains.
3) Sniff around. Musty, sweet, and odors that smell of raw beef may indicate infestation.
4) When lodging away from home (e.g. in hotels), check bed crevices and folds, as well as furniture or fixtures near the bed. Keep your luggage off the floor. Use the luggage rack in the room to place luggage upon.

Here are the top five actions to take if bedbugs are found:

1) Don't address the problem yourself. Contact building management or a licensed pest control professional with the tools and techniques to attack the bedbugs where they live, without unnecessarily exposing occupants to pesticide residues.
2) Vacuum floors, baseboards, and other bedbug-friendly locations often. Discard the vacuum bag or its contents immediately after it is collected.
3) Periodically recheck the cracks, crevices, and other locations where bedbugs have previously been found to ensure that they have not returned.
4) If you suspect a bite, contact a physician for authoritative confirmation that it resulted from a bedbug.
5) Limit visitors until the problem is gone.

Detection

If bedbugs are seen on the mattress, capture them and secure them in a vial or specimen container. Tape the container's lid for identification. Add rubbing alcohol or hand sanitizer to the container, which will kill the bug. Contact a licensed pest management company for identification and extermination.

The Patient

He or she may need to be moved to another bedroom. The following steps must be taken prior to moving the patient to another bedroom:

Place all the patient's clothing in a sealed, clear plastic bag. These items must be washed in hot water and dried for twenty minutes on the hottest temperature setting of the dryer to kill bedbugs and bedbug eggs.

Treatment and Control

Never remove any items from the bedbug-infested room before inspection and treatment by a licensed pest management professional. This will help to prevent relocating bedbugs to other areas within the premises. Contact a licensed management professional to perform a detailed bedbug inspection. Make available to the pest management professional all rooms adjacent to the infested room, as well as storage rooms, vacuum cleaners, hallways, and laundry rooms, for bedbug inspection and treatment where necessary. The pest management professional will determine if treatment is required. Comply with the pest management professional's instructions on how to prepare the room for bedbug eradication. In some instances, moving beds and other furnishings may be necessary.

Management of Furnishings and Other Materials Infested with Bedbugs

Do not remove from the room any infested materials designated for disposal. The room must be inspected and treated by the pest management professional. All clothing, linens, and materials designated for disposal from a bedbug-infested room are to be sealed in plastic bags to prevent relocating bedbugs to other areas within the premises. Dispose of all vacuumed refuse from the infested room in a plastic bag, including the vacuum cleaner bag. Do not unnecessarily dispose of mattresses and furniture. Have the pest management professional service all the furniture and mattresses. After treatment, any items marked for disposal should be wrapped in a protective cover, such as a bed sheet or plastic, before removing them from the infested room for transport to the disposal site. This cover should be clearly marked as bedbug-infested prior to disposing of the items, recycling the items, or placing items curbside.

Prevention

Place a waterproof mattress cover over the mattress.

Integrate bedbug monitoring into regular cleaning routines.

Weekly, monitor for evidence when changing the bed sheets. Also check the mattress and the edges of the mattress.

Quarterly, conduct thorough inspections of potential harborage locations: behind pictures and headboards and in furniture, including sofas and chairs.

Visit the EPA's bedbug website for more information.

As a prospective caregiver, you should know that the young, the elderly, the homebound, and those who are confined to bed are the most vulnerable to bug and/or rodent infestations arising from a lack of cleanliness. The foregoing information should be taken very seriously, especially for those in our society who depend on us as caregivers to take care of them.

Following are more suggestions for keeping the premises clean:

- Check the refrigerator for cleanliness. Check for open containers and spoiled food. Discard all spoiled food.
- Check the pantry and other places for food storage. Any open containers or food items that are past the sell-by date are to be discarded. Check all eating and cooking utensils for cleanliness. Make sure they are rust-free. Discard all cooking and eating utensils that are rusted.
- Check all drains and toilets in the house to make sure they are all in good operating condition. Address any toilet or drain that is not operating properly as soon as possible.

- Check for any unopened mail and any open mail that has not been attended to. This is a sign that the person for whom you provide care may need your assistance.
- Check the entire house for cleanliness.
- Make sure all faucets in the kitchen and bathroom(s) are working properly.
- Make sure the heating and air-conditioning system, along with the gas or electric range, is working properly.
- Check for rodents, droppings, and other pests within the house, alive or dead.

After reviewing the checklist, you may find that 90 percent of the items on the checklist are in serious need of assistance. I went through this with my mother. The first thing you need to do when approaching the person about his or her situation is to have your checklist in hand. With your list, you are ready to have a serious talk with the person for whom you provide care. Approach this subject very carefully and in a very gentle manner. Sometimes the elderly and the mentally challenged are very protective of their independence and resent anyone coming into their domain and finding fault or criticizing their living conditions. I approached the situation like this: "Mom, I've taken an inventory of the house, and I found some things a little out of order. Let me give you some examples: The laundry is not being addressed, there are dishes in the sink, your bed is not being changed on a regular basis, and the mail has not been opened for days. It looks like you have not been taking care of yourself very well. That really concerns me. You have not been taking your medication as directed, and I don't think you are eating enough to get the correct amount of the nutrients your body needs. With that being said, I would like to help you with all these things, along with any other issues that may arise. I am here to help you and to make sure you stay in the best of health. As your daughter, I believe that this is the time for me to take care of you. You did a wonderful job of loving and taking care of us, making sacrifices for us, and making sure we were provided with everything we needed and most of the things we wanted. I just want to say thank you for all you've done over the years for us. I love you, and I care about your health and welfare. I don't want anything to happen to you. That's why it's time for me to take care of you."

Explain in detail how you would like to help accomplish this task with the permission of the person for whom you provide care. After you have this conversation with the person, and once all parties are in agreement with you about getting things back in order, it's time to get to work.

CHAPTER 2

After Becoming a Caregiver

There are things that need to be addressed as soon as possible. The first of these is the mail. Collect all the mail and organize it in terms of priority. Address all pieces of mail according to the level of priority.

Next, obtain the names, addresses, and phone and fax numbers of the following providers:

- Health care providers
- Social worker
- Pharmacy
- Mobility wheelchair provider (if applicable)
- Utility companies—water, electric, gas and phone.

Health Care Providers

Before getting started, you will need to have a conversation with the person you will be caring for. This conversation should address the fact that he or she will have to allow you to obtain certain information on his or her behalf.

The information you will be obtaining will come from agencies, health care providers, pharmacies, and other places whose permission you may need to access the personal information of the person for whom you provide care. The person you will be caring for needs to provide permission for you to obtain information on his or her behalf regarding the status of his or her health and to ask questions regarding medication.

The primary care physician (PCP) is the first line of defense. This doctor will provide information to the other health professionals and will also provide referrals. Other health care providers confer with the PCP with regard to blood work and the overall health of the patient. Optometrists, dentists, podiatrists, and any and all other specialized health care providers contact the PCP of the person for whom you provide care to retrieve medical information. Obtain all health care providers' information: name, specialty, address, and phone and fax numbers. Place a call to all the health care providers of the person for whom you provide care and introduce yourself as his or her caregiver, also providing a contact number where you can be reached at any time.

The **primary care physician** is seen on average every six months, provided there are no complaints, questions, or concerns. The **optometrist** is seen on average every six months, provided there are no complaints, questions, or concerns. The **dentist** is seen twice a year for cleaning and X-rays if the person for whom you provide care does not wear dentures, and once a year if he or she does wear dentures—provided there are no complaints, questions, or concerns. The **podiatrist** is seen every twelve weeks, provided there are no complaints, questions, or concerns. If the person for whom you provide care has a social worker, utilize this individual's services and expertise. A social worker can be very helpful and resourceful. If you cannot find a name or a phone number for a social worker for the person for whom you provide care after looking through his or her paperwork, then you may want to contact the agency that oversees services for children, disabled people, and the elderly. The title of this agency may be the Department of Family and Children Services, although the name may vary from state to state. Once you have obtained a contact number for this department, call and identify yourself as the caregiver for the person for whom you provide care, then ask if the person to whom you are speaking is a social worker. If so, provide the person with phone numbers where you can be reached. If the social worker doesn't have a case file then explain your concerns regarding the person for whom you provide care and ask if he or she will need a social worker to qualify for services from this department.

Pharmacy

Retrieve the phone number and/or address of the pharmacy from any prescription bottles. Call the pharmacy and ask about the procedure for filing a prescription by phone or in person. Most pharmacies will allow you to call in refills utilizing the prescription number and the pharmacy phone number located on the bottle, provided there are refills left for the prescription (the number of refills is printed on each bottle). If the bottle says that authorization is required for a refill, then you or the pharmacy will need to contact the prescriber. The prescriber's name is located on the bottle. If the person for whom you provide care has been utilizing this pharmacy for all his or her prescriptions, then his or her insurance information will be on file and you will not have to present it each time you place an order or pick up a prescription. In some cases a Doctor can call in a new prescription. If any medications the person for whom you provide care for has a narcotic prescription, you must have a photo ID to obtain this medication, and you will have to sign for it. When contacting the pharmacy by phone or in person regarding picking up a prescription or obtaining information about a prescription for the person for whom you provide care, you will need to provide his or her first and last name and date of birth. Then and only then you will be allowed to obtain information regarding his or her prescription, including dosage amount, side effects, and the cost.

Mobility Chair Provider

If the person for whom you provide care has a mobility wheelchair, then you should contact this provider, introduce yourself as the caregiver for the person for whom you provide care, and give a contact number where you can be reached other than the home phone number. If the person for whom you provide care does not have a mobility chair and is in need of one, contact a mobility chair provider. Introduce yourself as the person's caregiver, and state the reason for your call, which is to get information about the process for obtaining a mobility chair for the person for whom you provide care. The mobility chair provider will send you all the information and paperwork needed for obtaining a mobility chair if the person for whom you provide care qualifies for one.

Utility Companies

You may want to contact all the companies providing utilities for the residence of the person for whom you provide care. However, before speaking to any utility company, you will have to get permission from the person for whom you provide care to speak to do so on his or her behalf. After getting permission from the person for whom you provide care to obtain information about the utilities on his or her behalf, you are now ready to contact the utility companies. Make sure the person for whom you provide care is in the same room with you before dialing the number. Place the call, introduce yourself as the caregiver, and then explain the reason for your call. The customer service representative will inform you that he or she cannot release any information regarding the account of the person for whom you provide care without obtaining permission. Inform the rep that the person has given you permission to speak on his or her behalf. Now you can proceed with obtaining information about his or her account. Remember, if the person for whom you provide care is disabled, is receiving Social Security, or is sixty-five or older, then he or she may qualify for a discount. Most of these companies offer a discount if the person qualifies in one or more of the above-mentioned categories. However, you must ask for the discount. In my experience, the utility company will not volunteer that type of information. The companies to contact are the water department, the electric company, the gas company, and the phone company.

Next up are tips about the following topics:

- Prescriptions, other medications, and supplements
- Transportation
- Diet
- Personal hygiene
- Oral hygiene
- Mobility
- Maintaining the exterior of the residence
- Cleaning the house

Prescriptions, Other Medications, and Supplements

Collect all medication bottles and check for the name of the medication, the milligrams or micrograms, the dosage, and the time of day and/or night the medication is to be taken. For medications in pill form, check for number of pills that are prescribed, located on the bottle, and for the number of refills, also located on the bottle. Keep all medication in a safe and secure place. If any supplements are on hand, find out when and why they were acquired and who suggested these supplements to be taken. A supplement may have been recommend by the primary care physician of the person for whom you provide care. Find out. Retrieve all medical insurance and prescription cards, and keep them in a safe place for easy access. Make sure all medical insurance and prescription cards have the correct spelling of the name of the person for whom you provide care.

Transportation

If you have suitable, reliable, and accessible transportation for the person for whom you provide care, then you are in good shape. If you don't, you may want to contact a transport service, whether public or private. In most cities, the public transportation system may offer special transportation for the elderly and the disabled. If your city offers this service, a discounted rate may apply for the elderly and the disabled, and in some cases you may ride for free with the person as the caregiver. The private transportation sector will charge a fee, or in most cases, the insurance company of the person for whom you provide care will cover the cost of transportation for him or her only. You can obtain this information from public and private sectors of transportation in your area that may offer transportation for the elderly and the disabled.

Diet

The primary care doctor, who oversees the general health of the person for whom you provide care and makes referrals if needed, would be the contact person for information regarding a special diet for the person for whom you provide care. If a special diet is needed, retrieve help from the primary care physician to devise a menu. A dietitian may be a part of the primary care physician's staff, or the doctor may recommend a dietitian to help you get started. Prepare a weekly menu from the items on the list. Menu preparation should include the input of the person for whom you provide care. A lot of ideas for recipes and preparation of foods can be obtained from a dietitian, books, magazines, family, and friends, and just by interacting with other caregivers. These sources will also help you to develop your own menu. The menu can be changed from week to week just by changing the food items around.

Oh, you must not forget fluid intake on a daily basis. Make sure the person for whom you provide care is drinking enough fluids, especially water. Make sure he or she is not restricted in daily fluid intake and that he or she is not retaining any fluid. This may be achieved by checking the hands, feet, legs, and face. Swollen feet and legs, and/or puffiness in the face, may be a sign of fluid retention. Make sure you document this information. Monitor the situation for at least seven days. If the person for whom you provide care is retaining fluid or not drinking enough fluid during this seven-day stretch, contact his or her primary care physician at once to set up an appointment.

Personal Hygiene

Purchase disposable gloves; keep these items on hand at all times. You will need these items if you have to assist in any area of personal hygiene. Disposable gloves are essential; they are not only for your protection, but also for the protection of the person you are caring for. Wearing gloves will prevent you from transmitting anything to the person for whom you provide care. It will also prevent him or her from transmitting anything to you. It takes only one time of failing to wear disposable gloves to cause a very serious health concern for you or the person you are caring for. The rule of thumb is always to protect yourself and the one you are caring for.

Make sure bathing is performed daily. Sometimes bathing may become necessary more than once a day. This will depend on the physical condition of the person you care for. If he or she wears disposable undergarments, his or her body should be washed after every change of the disposable undergarments. Make sure a water barrier ointment is placed on the person's bottom after washing. If this process is not performed, then the person's skin may break down. If sores occur, contact the person's primary care physician at once. This is why personal hygienic practices are imperative, to prevent infections and other sores.

Oral Hygiene

This should be performed in the morning and in the evening before bedtime. Dentures should be soaked in a denture solution in a special denture container overnight. Dentures have a special brush for cleaning. You can be obtain one from any store that carries cleaning and storage supplies for dentures.

Mobility

After observing the person for whom you provide care, you should have a clear idea of how mobile he or she is. If he or she utilizes a walker, a manual wheelchair, or a mobility wheelchair, make sure all mobility items are in good condition, are working properly, and are cleaned on a regular basis. Make sure to remove all throw rugs from bedrooms, the living area, and bathrooms so as to eliminate potential tripping hazards.

Maintaining the Exterior of the Residence

If the person for whom you provide care utilizes a mobile chair or a walker, and if there is more one entrance/exit to the house, make sure at least one of the entrances has a ramp for a mobility chair, wheelchair, or walker. Contact the Department on Aging and Disabilities. They can direct you to resources that may assist you with a ramp if one is needed, depending on which area of the country you reside in.

Lawn care and snow and ice removal are both very important. Look into hiring a reliable, trustworthy, and reasonable person or company for the purpose of maintaining the lawn in season and out of season. Snow and ice removal in the winter months is just as important. You may want to get referrals from neighbors, from online, or in the want ads.

Cleaning the House

When cleaning a house, you may need the assistance of a cleaning company. This will depend on the size of the house and the number of rooms. Make sure every room in the house is clean, including closets and other areas of storage.

CHAPTER 3

Organization

The first thing you must do is to bring organization, discipline, and structure into your own life. If you don't have structure and discipline, you will likely experience disorganization, anxiety, sleeplessness, lack of concentration, and restlessness, and perhaps a decrease or increase in appetite. All these things can cause stress, which can lead to illness. You don't want to transfer your stress to the person you are caring for or to develop any illnesses yourself. This is why I cannot stress enough the importance of getting organized and staying organized. When a caregiver is organized, this will transfer to the person he or she is providing care for. It's a trickle-down effect. When you become organized and stay organized, this will help the person you are caring for with his or her mental and physical stability, adding to his or her feeling of safety and security. If for any reason you are no longer this person's caregiver, this will give him or her a sense of knowing what to expect from a caregiver and what not to except from a caregiver. You will have already developed a structure and guidelines for the person to expect.

The Living Area

Better known as the living room, this is the first room people will enter when they come into the residence. This room should be immaculate and clutter-free at all times. There should never be carpets or throw rugs in this room—or in any room in the residence. If the person for whom you provide care is able to access this room at any time by way of walker, crutches, or a wheelchair, then any carpeting or throw rugs may be very dangerous, an accident waiting to happen. Bare floors are best for anyone needing the assistance of any mobility aids.

Bedroom

Organization of this room is essential, as it is important for the rest of the person for whom you provide care. Relaxing, sleeping, and rejuvenating aid in the body's process of healing itself and may help to restore the health of the person for whom you provide care. Cleanness is imperative, as is functionality. Do not clutter the bedroom with unnecessary things. When a bedroom is cluttered and disorganized, it can have a negative effect on a person's mental and emotional state. Do not clutter the bedroom with unnecessary furniture; use only furniture that is functional.

Look at the floor space. If the person for whom you provide care utilizes a walker, crutches, a manual wheelchair, or a mobility chair, too many unnecessary items in the bedroom can cause clutter that can result in an accident. I have found that carpet is the worst thing to have in a house where there is a sick person. Carpet collects dirt and dust, which can cause allergies, and if the carpet gets wet, mold can grow. Bare floors are the best, as they are more sanitary and easier to maintain. Never place throw rugs on any floor, carpeted or bare, as throw rugs are not friendly to those who utilize a walker, a wheelchair, or a mobility chair.

This room should have a chest of drawers for storing sleepwear and other personal items, and at least one night table with drawers that will support a phone and a lamp. This night table might house the favorite books of the person for whom you provide care and other personal items he or she may want to have readily available.

Check how much space is available in the bedroom closets for hanging clothes. Measure the space. Check how much overhead shelf space is available in the closets for storing bed linens, towels, washcloths, and blankets. If there is no linen closet and if overhead shelving is applicable, measure that space for open-storage concepts (open-storage concepts for linens, towels, and washcloths are perfect). Purchase space bags for storing seasonal blankets, comforters, and clothing, then store these items under the bed. These are space savers that will keep out dust, dirt, and moisture. In addition to storing them under beds, they may also be stored in closets, attics, basements, or garages.

Bathrooms

Make sure all bathrooms are clean and that fixtures and showerheads are in good operating condition. Make sure the bathtub drain and all sink drains are open and operating properly. Make sure the toilet is operating and in good condition. If the person for whom you provide care is mobile enough to utilize the bathroom, make sure the toilet seat is the correct height. You may need to get a higher toilet seat and a shower bench for him or her to sit upon when taking a shower, and perhaps install bars that will provide support when entering and exiting the shower. Make sure any bars installed in the bathroom are weight-bearing only.

Laundry Area

If there is a washer and dryer, make sure both are in good operating condition. If they are not working and the cost of getting them repaired is too high, replace them. Obtain these items as soon as possible. Purchase an energy-saving washer and dryer. This will help to lower utility bills (electric, gas, and water).

Kitchen

Make sure this area is clean and clutter-free. If this is an eat-in kitchen or a dining room, there should be enough room for any mobility aid to function without any obstruction. Make sure the range/oven and refrigerator/freezer are clean and in good operating condition. Remove all expired and spoiled foods from the refrigerator. Remove all expired food from the pantry and other storage areas in the kitchen that may house nonperishable foods. Check the kitchen cabinets for chipped dishes, cups, and glasses. These items should be discarded. All aluminum pots should be discarded. It is unhealthy for cooking.

Paperwork

You will be receiving a lot of important papers that should be readily available at all times. They should be organized and in a safe place. Locate a place in the residence that is out of sight, if possible. Obtain a two-drawer file cabinet for hanging file holders and manila files. Obtain a computer armoire for housing a combo printer, copier, and fax machine and a tablet or laptop. In this day and age, these tools of technology are essential. These items will make you much more efficient as a caregiver. The reason I suggest a tablet or laptop is because of the portability from room to room. And you can travel with a tablet or a laptop.

The printer will print information from your computer. The copier will make copies of documents. You can send attachments through your email account when and if necessary. Also obtain a memory stick to save information from your computer. A computer armoire will have storage for a printer/copier and fax machine and storage for any office supplies that you will need, such as writing pads, pencils, pens, paper clips, rubber bands, a stapler and staples, a Scotch tape dispenser, tape, and a calculator. You will need a small pocket calendar and a flat desk/wall calendar, this will help you stay organized with regard to the appointments of the person for whom you provide care and other important information you may need to see at a glance. You can obtain all these supplies from any office supply store. You should have a file for each health care professional, a file for each organization you may be communicating with, and a separate file for each utility company's notices and bills. You will be surprised to learn how much paperwork you receive when caring for someone. When discarding paperwork with personal information, such as bank statements, do so with safety from identity theft in mind. Make sure to keep all paperwork safe and organized.

CHAPTER 4

Documentation

Documentation is very important. When interacting with local, state, or federal agencies, you may have to complete paperwork on behalf of the person you are caring for. These documents are to be accurate and available upon request. Documentation may come from utility companies, doctors' offices, hospitals, and any agency you come in contact with involving the person you are caring for. The reason for attending to any documentation is to ensure that the person for whom you provide care is receiving the best service he or she is entitled to. Mistakes can happen, and errors in paperwork may occur within any agency. This is why it is your responsibility to make sure all documentation is current and accurate at all times, to the best of your ability. Keep an updated list of the following documentation. The most efficient way to achieve this is to have a list of the items below in Microsoft Word. When this information is updated, print out any changes and keep the paperwork in a safe place.

Make sure you have a printed list in Word form of the following:

- All hospital visits, including name of the hospital, the dates of any stays, the dates of admission and discharge, the reason for the visit, and the treatment undergone.

- All doctor appointments, including name of doctor, date, time, and reason for visit.
- All surgeries, including type of surgery, the name of the hospital, and the city and state in which the hospital is located.
- All doctors and dentists, including name, specialty, phone number, and address.
- Pharmacy, including address and phone number.
- All medication taken, including name, dosage (usually in milligrams), frequency (how many times a day it is taken), what time of day it is to be taken (morning, noon, afternoon, or evening), reason for taking the medication, the date the person started taking the medication, and the name of the prescribing doctor.

When visiting a hospital, ER, or doctor's office, make sure you provide them with a updated list of all medications; the name, address, and phone number of the pharmacy; the name of the primary care physician, including address and phone number; and the names of all other physicians who are caring for the person for whom you provide care. Make sure you have the ID of the person for whom you provide care, along with insurance information and insurance cards. Keep all these items in a safe place so they are readily available. If you are not in the habit of carrying a pen/pencil and writing tablet with you, then get in the habit now, because you never know whom you may come in contact with.

Make sure you have a reliable cell phone. Store all important phone numbers in your cell phone. Give your cell number, as well as the home phone number where you can be reached. When interacting with persons or agencies on behalf of the person you are caring for, it's very important that you document all communication. You will be communicating a lot by phone, as well as in person, so make sure you get the person's name, the name of the organization/

agency, and the date and time of the conversation. Do this both when placing calls and receiving calls.

When you follow this procedure for documentation, it will help you to track any appointments, any procedures, and all conversations regarding the person you are caring for. If for any reason you have any concerns regarding the person you are caring for, this procedure will help you. When you have this information on hand, you will be surprised how you are treated. People will sit up and take notice of your accuracy and professionalism. Trust me, you will be treated as a professional. For more information, see Chapter 16: Tips.

CHAPTER 5

Time Management

Time management is very important, especially for a caregiver. What does this mean? Well, let's see. Time management is when you manage the time you have in the most productive way possible to accomplish and address what is needed. This process will not only benefit you but will also benefit the person you are caring for. Time management can make or break appointments. Getting the person for whom you provide care ready for an appointment, or just getting him or her ready for daily activities, dispensing medication, making a menu, preparing meals, food shopping/house whole shopping, doing the housecleaning, doing the laundry, vacuuming, dusting, helping him or her bathe, aiding in getting him or her dressed (if application), and spending time with him or her all require time management. You should know and have a list of things that need to be addressed the day before. You must learn to value, manage, and make the most of your time. You must learn to prioritize everything you do on a daily basis. Having the responsibility of doing all the foregoing things—and much more—will compel you to conform to a time schedule. Failure to managing your time as a caregiver will result in your worst nightmare coming true. Haste makes waste.

CHAPTER 6

Live-In Caregiver

A live-in caregiver has an awesome responsibility. You have to be available almost twenty-four hours a day. Of course, this depends upon the health concerns of the person you are caring for. As a live-in caregiver, you will be living with the person you are caring for, or he or she will be living with you. The person you are caring for will become your first and foremost concern. As a live-in caregiver you will be expected to be reliable, dependable, responsible, trustworthily, considerate, thoughtful, loving, and kind. There will be times when you will become overwhelmed with the responsibility of being a caregiver; however, the rewards of your achievements will outweigh the feeling of being overwhelmed you may get from time to time. Your greatest reward will be in how well you perform as a caregiver. This will show up in the physical appearance, performance, and mental stability of the person you are caring for. Whatever the living situation, read and follow the instructions in the chapters on organization (chapter 3), documentation (chapter 4), and time management (chapter 5) to become the very best caregiver you can be. To avoid the feeling of being overwhelmed, seek help. There are local and state agencies available to help you. Contact them before you get to the point of being overwhelmed.

CHAPTER 7
Nursing Home Caregiver

Most people don't know that a caregiver may provide care for a person who resides in a nursing home. If you are responsible for well-being in most aspects of the life of someone who lives in a nursing home, then you are considered a nursing home caregiver. A nursing home caregiver has almost same responsibilities as a live-in caregiver does. You should go to the nursing home every day. You should check the room of the person for whom you provide care to make sure it has been cleaned and that the bed linens are clean. You should check to make sure all the individual's personal belongings are there. You should check his or her physical body for any sores, swelling, or discoloration. You should ask if he or she has been bathed that day. You should ask if he or she has any activities scheduled that day. You should check the menu on every visit to the nursing home and become knowledgeable with regard to the eating habits of the person for whom you provide care. You should ask if he or she has eaten all or most of all his or her meals. You should inquire about his or her medication, asking if new medication has been prescribed, if any current medication has been stopped, or there has been an increase or decrease in the dosage since your last visit. Ask if any physical routine has been added or taken away since your last visit.

All the foregoing concerns can be addressed at the nurses' station. Always ask questions out of concern and not to make any accusation. Make sure you have pen and paper on hand, and always make a note of the person's name, the person's title, and the date and time you spoke with the person. Obtaining this information is very important.

My experience with nursing home procedures includes having monthly meetings with the following: doctor, dietitian, head nurse, social worker, and activities coordinator. Each of these people will give you a progress report with regard to the condition of the person for whom you provide care and recommendations if needed. If you have not been approached regarding any meetings pertaining to the person you are caring for, then request a meeting with all these personnel. These meetings will help you to stay informed of the progress made by the person for whom you provide care. Or if the individual is failing to make progress, the meetings will afford you the opportunity to ask questions, express concerns, and offer suggestions regarding the care of the person for whom you are responsible.

Most nursing homes offer personal grooming for their residents. This may come at an additional cost. The personal care offered may include haircuts, hair grooming, pedicures, and manicures. Check with the admissions coordinator. The person for whom you provide care may have personal items that you have provided. Make sure you label all personal items with his or her name.

You may want to purchase additional pillows, pillowcases, blankets, socks, and sleeping attire. With regard to sleeping attire, a hospital gown may be required. Check with the nursing staff. Make sure you launder these items yourself. Request a laundry basket if the nursing home provides one, or purchase one yourself. Place the name of the person for whom you provide care on his/her laundry basket. Inform all personnel that you will be doing his or her laundry.

Purchase natural toothpaste, natural soap (body wash or bar soap), natural moisturizing lotion that can be applied to the face and body, and natural shampoo and hair conditioner. These natural products have no harmful agents. They will not dry the skin. Make sure you place the name of the person for whom you provide care on all items belonging to him or her. In chapter 16, I provide tips for where you can obtain these products.

After purchasing items for the bed of the person for whom you provide care and his or her personal attire, you will want to launder these yourself. For any other items belonging to him or her, for example, radio, CD player, TV, or headphones, take a black marker and use it to write his or her name on these items. Place clear tape over the name. Items may be lost or misplaced in any nursing home, physical rehabilitation facility, or hospital facility or if the person for whom you provide care has to relocate to another room or another facility.

Every week, purchase fresh-cut flowers for the person for whom you provide care. Also purchase a green plant that is easy to care for. You would be surprised to see how such little things can make a difference in the life of someone living in a nursing home.

If the diet of the person for whom you provide care permits, take him or her a special treat, something that he or she likes, at least once a week. These special offerings make the person feel special, loved, cared for, and not forgotten. Being in a nursing home can make a person feel isolated from family and friends. To the best of your ability, make sure the person for whom you provide care does not experience this feeling. Make the person feel as if he or she is at home as much as possible. You can also make this possible by encouraging family and friends to visit as often as possible.

Last but not least, make sure your visit is at least an hour, if not longer. Talk with the person for whom you provide care. Ask questions, for example: "How was your day?" "Did you enjoy your meals?" "What did you have for breakfast, lunch, and dinner?" "What did you have to drink today?" "Did you have dessert?" "Did you get a bath today?" "Tell me what you did not like today regarding your meals, or any other concerns you may have." Make sure you encourage the person to participate in activities, especially physical activities if possible.

CHAPTER 8

Caregiver for the Mentally Challenged

In this chapter, I discuss my experience as caregiver for the mentally challenged. Let me give you a little background first. The person I was caring for was my brother, who is five years older than I. He attended a special secondary school and then attended a special vocational school. He worked for most of his adult life, until he was no longer able to function mentally at work. My mother was his caregiver until her health failed and she could no longer do the job. I assumed responsibility as his caregiver until his death. He had the ability to bathe, feed, and dress himself. His chores involved doing the dishes and keeping his room clean. However, he did not have the capability to exercise, to follow through with good sound judgment, or to handle his financial affairs.

I share this story with you to let you know that you can care for a mentally challenged person who has the same challenges as my brother. To do so requires a great deal of patience. My brother needed something to keep him occupied at all times. He needed social interaction. We would go out to dinner every Friday, something he looked forward to doing. He loved watching television, listening to music, and dancing. We would attend a social event at least once a month so he could dance.

Taking care of my brother with the type of challenges he had helped me to grow as a person. Mentally challenged people have to feel wanted and needed. They need to feel and know that they are useful. For example, they often want to have responsibility for chores such as washing dishes, making sure the bathroom is clean, taking out the trash, and getting the mail from the mailbox. Going out to dinner at least once a week and taking day trips or long-distance trips is excellent for them. They enjoy the interaction with people.

To care for someone who is mentally challenged, you must exercise firmness, love, and kindness. Just because the person is challenged mentally does not in any way excuse bad behavior. When the person for whom you provide care behaves poorly, you must bring this to his or her attention in a kind, gentle, and loving manner. Remember, you are the caregiver and you are in control. From time to time, you have to reaffirm this.

The information I have outlined here is not intended for all cases with a mentally challenged person. The foregoing information relates to my own personal experience in caring for someone with a mental illness. It is not meant to be inclusive for all those who suffer from mental illness.

CHAPTER 9

Non-Live-In Caregiver

A non-live-in caregiver is the same as a caregiver for a person who resides in a nursing home or for someone who does not reside with his or her caregiver, either in his or her own house or in the home of the caregiver. If you are a non-live-in caregiver, you have to apply the same principles as discussed in Chapter 7: Nursing Home Caregiver. Serving as this type of caregiver can be very challenging because you are not living with the person for whom you provide care and he or she is not living with you. The only way this will work is if you live next door, within walking distance, or in the same apartment building. This type of caregiving is for a person who is mobile and can get around pretty much on his or her own and is able to bathe himself or herself, feed himself or herself, and go the bathroom on his or her own; he or she just needs some assistance with meals, medication, checking incoming mail, making sure appointments are made, making sure appointments are kept, and last but not least, making sure he or she receives the companionship he or she needs.

Just keep in mind that this type of caregiving can be very stressful. The first reason for this is that you have to leave your residence to take care of the person, which can become quite challenging. There will be days when you will find it difficult to go and make sure the person for whom you provide care is okay. You will begin to make excuses for not going to check on him or her. You may begin to miss days of checking on him or her. You may begin to feel that the responsibility is a little more than you can handle. I believe this is the most challenging and the most stressful part of being a non-live-in caregiver. You may begin to limit your visits. Before this begins to happen, please make sure you have an emergency plan in place. The person you are caring for will need to have access to you 24/7. He or she needs a phone number where you can be reached at all times. You should think it through very carefully before deciding to become a non-live-in caregiver.

Part II

TAKING CARE
OF YOURSELF

As a person who served as a caregiver for a long time, I had to learn through trial and error how to take care of myself. Taking care of yourself has to be your number one priority. To become the most capable and effective caregiver you can be, this is a must. You must stay in the best of health physically, mentally, and emotionally. Caregiving is an awesome responsibility. A caregiver has to know how to take care of himself or herself. Then and only then will he or she be in the position to care for someone else.

By taking care of ourselves, we demonstrate our capability for caring for someone else. When we are taking care of ourselves, it is evident in our physical appearance, in our mental sharpness, and in our emotional state. Our thinking is clearer, and these clear thought patterns are evidenced by the things we do and how we accomplish them. Our attention to detail will be recognized in our work as a caregiver. We need to have the best diet possible. We need to exercise, to get the correct amount of rest and sleep, and to take time for ourselves. I would recommend meditation. Meditation, when performed on a daily basis, can help lower blood pressure and cause a person to stay focused, remain centered, and stay grounded. You may find information on meditation at your local library or your favorite bookstore.

All the things I've mentioned here will also give you more confidence, better self-assurance, and a greater sense of accomplishment. Being a caregiver can be very stressful, so look for the hummer in everything. Laughter is the best stress buster. It lowers the blood pressure. It's good for the heart and simply makes a person feel great.

There will be times when you may feel the need to talk to someone. Perhaps you will reach out a friend or an organization in your area that provides services for caregivers who are in need of support. Become your own advocate when it comes to taking care of yourself. No one can do this better than you. Remember: live, laugh, love!

CHAPTER 10

Making Sure You Are in Good Health

I have been a caregiver for a long time. I know the importance of taking care of oneself. It is a must to be and to stay in the best of health. The best of health includes physical, emotional, and mental health. If you have any concerns regarding your health, address them as soon as possible.

As caregivers, we have to learn the art of listening to what our bodies are telling us. Our bodies let us know when something is not right. The human body never fails to communicate and keep you informed when something is wrong. If you have any concerns, by all means seek out your health care provider to help you address the health concerns you have. You must reach out and get the support you need. You don't have to feel that you are alone during this process of caregiving. Remember, staying in good health makes for an excellent caregiver!

CHAPTER 11

Getting Proper Nutrition

Getting the proper nutrition your body needs on a daily basis is required. You may not be getting enough nutrients from the foods you eat. Taking a good-quality daily supplement may be the answer. A good daily supplement should contain minerals. Minerals are needed for nail growth, hair growth, and maintaining healthy teeth and healthy bones. Eating nutrient-dense foods in conjunction with taking supplements is not only important but also imperative. A healthy weight is a very important component as well.

The human body requires a lot of things: protein, carbohydrates, fats, minerals and vitamins. These nutrients can be found in fruits, dairy, and vegetables. Healthy snacks on hand at home are an excellent choice. A caregiver should carry healthy snacks with him or her. Some examples of healthy snacks are unsalted nuts, baby carrots, apples, bananas, whole grain crackers, and low-fat cheese. Read food labels. The label will indicate the correct portion size. Eating the proper portions will also help with weight control.

The other component in making sure you are staying healthy is to drink enough water. Drinking enough water will keep you hydrated. Drinking enough water will also help you from becoming constipated.

As people grow older, we need vitamin supplements and minerals in our diet. Remember, a healthy and energized caregiver is the best caregiver.

CHAPTER 12

Getting Enough Rest

Rest is not sleep. You may fall and stay asleep; however, you may not be getting enough rest while sleeping. Resting is when the mind is free of the clutter brought about by thinking about things such as appointments you forgot to make, grocery shopping you did not have time to complete, and phone calls you forgot to make. These things and more can create clutter in your mind, preventing you from getting the rest you need to function properly.

Before going to bed, make a list of all the things you wanted to accomplish during the course of the day but did not have an opportunity to do. This process will help to clear your mind of all those things that will keep you from resting. It is important to write these things down on paper. I find this method to be a lifesaver. Getting such things off my mind helps me to get a good night's rest. The proper amount of rest helps the mind and body to rejuvenate. Getting enough rest will help you to perform at your very best. If you are not getting enough rest, you may become the one receiving care!

CHAPTER 13

Getting Enough Sleep

Sleep may become very elusive and difficult to obtain—and very hard to retain. We all have the problem of not getting enough sleep and finding it difficult to stay asleep at some point and time in our lives. I have a few suggestions for getting to sleep and staying asleep:

Make sure you are sleeping on a good mattress. Your mattress should be no more than eight years old. Your mattress should be flipped once a month.

Remove clutter from your bedroom. This will help you get to sleep and stay asleep. When you remove clutter from your bedroom, you remove the clutter from your mind.

The temperature in your bedroom should be cool; you may want to crack a window for air ventilation. Try going to bed the same time every night. Have a good pillow to sleep on. Turn off all electronic devices, and don't sleep with your cell phone in the bed with you. Purchase a good sleep mask to help to block out any light that may filter into the bedroom. Having blackout drapes over your bedroom window will also keep outside light from entering the room.

Don't drink caffeine prior to going to bed. If you must have caffeine before going to bed, don't drink any three hours prior to bedtime.

You may want to do some transcendental meditation or some form of exercise. You may want to take a hot shower or bath and drink a cup of chamomile tea prior to bedtime. This can be done one hour before going to bed.

Seven hours of good sleep should be very beneficial. If you have to get up by six in the morning, then you should be in bed by ten at night. You should be sound asleep by eleven o'clock. By following this little tip, it should give you seven hours of good sleep.

After adopting these tips with regard to getting to sleep and staying asleep, you should be on your way to a good night's sleep. Try the foregoing suggestions for at least thirty days. If they do not work for you, then contact your health care provider. Remember, not getting enough sleep or getting poor-quality sleep may be detrimental to your health and likely will have an effect on your emotional, physical, and mental well-being. It might also interfere with your responsibilities as a caregiver.

CHAPTER 14

Getting Enough Exercise

Getting enough physical and mental exercise is very important for everyone, especially caregivers. Caregivers often have to bend, lift, squat, and pull in carrying out their duties. If you are not in the best physical condition to perform these tasks, then the physical components of caregiving will take a toll on your body. You must not allow this to happen. You have taken on the responsibility for caring for someone else.

The first thing you must do is to obtain the right clothing for exercising, including shoes for walking, outer garments for the same purpose, and support undergarments for the same purpose. There are a number of exercise routines I would recommend, as follows: (1) walking, which is easy and convenient; (2) water aerobics, which is very friendly on the joints and will not leave your muscles sore; (3) bike riding, which is also very good for the joints; (4) yoga, which is excellent for strengthening your body and our core (I did not mention jogging for this reason. I believe jogging can be very hard on the joints [ankles. knees and hips], especially for women; (5) tai chi, which will help with joints and will help you to maintain your balance; and (6) stretching before beginning any of these exercises. Stretching is excellent for keeping the body flexible.

Stretching gives you more flexibility and keeps you from shrinking as you get older. Have you ever known a person who was very tall and, when he or she got older, appeared to have gotten shorter? This is because the person's muscles shrank. My former chiropractor shared this information with me some years ago, along with the importance of stretching. A stretching routine has been working for me for many years. Remember, *stretch* and keep yourself moving.

CHAPTER 15

Getting Enough Me Time

Okay, what is me time? Me time is the time you take to care for yourself. You don't have to be a caregiver to give yourself me time. Taking time out for your self is very important. If you don't do this, especially as a caregiver, you may experience what is called burnout, meaning you are giving so much care to someone else that you are forgetting to care for yourself. If you burn out, you may be the one who is in need of receiving care.

I have some great things to share with you that work for me so that burnout will not happen to you. First, make sure you take the time to care for your crowning glory (your hair). Caring for one's hair tends to make one feel much better. Do this yourself, or go to a professional to get your crowning glory looking beautiful. Having this done will lift your spirits and make you look and feel great. Try some color in your hair as well; you will be surprised what a difference it will make. Do this at least once month or as often as you feel the need.

Make sure to keep your nails and feet looking their best at all times as well. Give yourself a manicure-pedicure or have a professional perform this service. Keeping your nails at a professional length, appropriate for a caregiver, is very important. In most cases, you will be utilizing hand sanitizer and gloves often. This is why it is a must to keep your nails at an appropriate length, for sanitary reasons.

Take a soak in the bathtub at least once a week. Give yourself a facial at least once a week. You may want to treat yourself to a massage every three months. Make sure to drink plenty of water after a massage. The massage will release toxins. Drinking water after the massage will remove the toxins from your body.

Getting Out

Schedule an outing at least once a month. (Go see a movie, go out for lunch or dinner, or just get together with friends.)

Staying Informed

Stay up to date with current events, locally and nationally. Keeping yourself informed helps your brain to function to the best of its ability and keeps your mind sharp. Stay informed of the most recent health information. Get fresh air at least once a day. All these things can be achieved within the space of one or two days; you just need to make a plan and a schedule. This not only will keep you looking and feeling well, but it will also keep your mental and emotional state intact. If you don't take care of yourself as a caregiver, you may find yourself at risk for health problems and emotional problems.

CHAPTER 16

Tips

I have some great tips that will help make your caregiving responsibilities more manageable, more efficient, and easier. Some of the tips that I will be sharing with you came from friends or relatives, and some are from my own life experiences as a caregiver.

When caring for yourself, the following things are a must:

- Washing hands
- Using disposable gloves
- Using hand sanitizer
- Wearing the right clothing
- Wearing the right shoes

Make sure you always wash your hands. Wear disposable gloves when aiding in personal grooming (e.g., shaving), bathing, changing undergarments, administering medication, and making any other form of personal contact with the person you are caring for. You should also utilize hand sanitizer after taking off disposable gloves. This will minimize cross-contamination between you and the person you are caring for. I would also recommend wearing scrubs during your caregiving duties. These items are comfortable, easy to care for, and in most cases stain-resistant.

Skin Care and Oral Care

Through trial and error, my journey of searching for the right bath and skin care products has led me to a number of products that work and are great for the mind, body, and spirit. *Do not* utilize products that contain the following ingredients: parabens, phthalates, paraffin, gluten, propylene glycol, mineral oil, synthetic fragrance, PABA, synthetic color, DEA, or sulfates. All the foregoing ingredients are very harmful to the skin and hair. The soaps, body washes, lotions, creams, and hair care products that contain such ingredients may smell good, and the packaging may be eye-appealing, but these ingredients are harmful to the skin and hair. I strongly recommend any one of the products made by SheaMoisture. I have been utilizing SheaMoisture products for the person I care for and for myself for a while. This line of products includes a variety of soaps, body washes, body oils, lotions, and hair care products with no harmful ingredients. Check out their website at www.SheaMoisture.com. All the products contain shea butter. You can purchase these products online or at some Walmart, Target, Ulta, and Walgreens stores. Also check out the website iherb.com; this company's products are available to order online only. This outlet offers not only bath, body, hair, and oral care products but also a variety of vitamin supplements. Nourish.com is another company that offers bath and body products for sale online ordering or in stores. They have bricks-and-mortar stores in the states of Georgia and Florida. This company also produces their own bath and body products, all of which contain shea butter. I recommend all three companies; I purchase from all three on a regular basis. A little goes a long way!

Shower and Exfoliate

Before soaking in the tub, take a shower. Utilize a good natural soap and exfoliating gloves every day to remove dead skin cells, which accumulate on the skin every seventy-two hours. These dead skin cells, if not removed, result in dirt accumulation and body odor. The exfoliating process will also help with blood circulation. When you exfoliate regularly, your skin will become soft and supple and will take on a glow. This is why it's important to exfoliate. The skin is the largest of the three eliminative organs, which eliminate toxins from the body. The other two organs are the liver and the kidneys. All three of these organs perform the job of eliminating waste from the body. Exfoliating can be done every time you take a shower. At least once a week, wash your exfoliating gloves in the washer along with any white clothes. In between the weekly laundering of your gloves in the washer, spray them with water and bleach solution after each use. Try these gloves. I promise you, they will leave your skin soft and smooth. The gloves can be purchased at any store that carries items for bath and body care.

Soaking the Body

Soaking the body in the bathtub is very relaxing. This process will help aching muscles by allowing them to relax. Soaking will also help ease any soreness in the joints. It will also aid in relaxing and may help induce sleep.

I used to purchase an over-the-counter salt bath soak, but I discovered that I was spending too much money on it. One day it came to me that I could make my own soaking solution. I read the label of the one I was using and found that the main ingredient is sea salt. I substituted coarse kosher salt for the sea salt.

Items needed to make your own bath soaking solution:

1 plastic jar (large enough to hold a three-pound box of coarse kosher salt)

1 three-pound box of coarse kosher salt

1 medium-size cotton drawstring bag

lavender leaves

1 scoop (metal or plastic)

label the container (optional)

Directions:

Pour the salt in the plastic container. Add four scoops of lavender to the salt mixture. Place the lid on the container. Shake the container with the salt and lavender mixture to evenly distribute the lavender.

Now you are ready to take a soak. Place about three scoops of the bath salts and lavender mixture into the cotton drawstring bag. Place this bag in a bath full of very warm water. Get in the tub and soak for at least thirty minutes, making sure the bathwater stays very warm. After soaking, remove the cotton bag from the tub. The salt will have dissolved in the water, and the lavender leaves will remain in the bag. Allow the cotton bag to dry completely, then discard the dry lavender. Place the dry cotton bag back in the container of coarse kosher salt and lavender leaves until you are ready for your next soak. Try this at least once a week. You will feel like a new person after each soak. Enjoy!

I have another tip I would like to share: No soap is needed when soaking in the tub. You are soaking your body to relieve sore muscles and aching joints and for relaxation. This process is not for washing your body.

Oral Care

I don't have dentures. The product I utilize for oral care is a natural toothpaste with no harmful ingredients. This product, which is SLS-free, fluoride-free, and gluten-free, is an antiplaque, whitening, tartar control toothpaste that encourages fresh breath. The name of this product is Jason, which can be found on the iherbs website or in stores that carry natural oral care products. A Jason oral product keeps your smile bright without harsh abrasives or irritating chemicals. Jason makes a great body wash as well. I have been using this product for over thirty years without any complaints.

Make sure you have a dental checkup every six months to address any concerns you may have about oral care.

Feet

You must make sure you take care of your feet. As a caregiver, I am on my feet a lot. You also need to wear a good shoe with support. I would recommend a good nursing shoe that has a good arch support. This type of shoe will also protect your feet. There are times when you may have to assist with physically transporting the person for whom you provide care from one place to another. If you don't wear the proper shoes, this can result in injury to your feet. Or you may develop joint problems with your ankles, knees, or hips. You might also cause pain or damage to your lower back. Take the time to do some research and get the correct footwear. Trust me, you don't want to create any physical health problems because you are not wearing the right shoe for the job.

As a caregiver, I strongly recommend wearing scrubs. Scrubs are comfortable and easily cleaned of any stains. I would recommend purchasing at least three tops and three bottoms to start with. I would recommend washing these items separately from your personal laundry. I would also recommend wearing a watch with a large face and large numbers. A watch with a big face and large numbers allows you to just glance at it to see what time it is.

Treat yourself to a pedicure, or do it yourself. I prefer to give myself a pedicure at least once a month. I utilize a pumice stone to keep my feet smooth and callus-free. I perform this process every time I take a shower, paying close attention to my heels and the balls of my feet. You may purchase a small kit to care for your feet from a beauty supply store.

Time Management

Time management is very important, especially for a caregiver. Failure to manage your time wisely can result in stress. This can make your life hectic, which may result in health problems. Stress is not good for you and not good for the person you are caring for. Let me give you some examples of how to complete things utilizing time increments of five, fifteen, and twenty minutes. This method will allow you to wisely maximize your time:

- In five minutes, you can prepare a grocery list.
- In five minutes, you can wash dishes for two (provided you rinse the dishes right after eating).
- In fifteen minutes, you can gather laundry and place it in in the washer. (Always utilize disposable gloves.)

- In fifteen minutes, you can fold laundry.
- In fifteen minutes, you can vacuum three rooms.
- In fifteen minutes, you can prepare breakfast.
- In fifteen minutes, you can clean two bathrooms.
- In twenty minutes, you can prepare three-quarters of your dinner.

The foregoing are just examples of what you can accomplish within any time frame you may have. The most important thing is to manage your time wisely and figure out what you can accomplish within that time frame. When time management is performed often and on a regular basis, it will become part of your daily routine. I utilize time management all the time. Managing your time well gives you more free time to enjoy.

Organization

The process of time management goes hand in hand with organization. You must be organized and stay organized. Without organization, caregiving can and will become very stressful. Everything in your life must be based on organization, from the time you awake to the time you go to bed. This will be the only way you will survive as a healthily and efficient caregiver and not become the person who needs to be taken care of.

Kitchen and Sickroom Receptacles, Including Laundry Baskets

In your kitchen, have a thirteen-gallon trash receptacle with a cover. A clean and fresh-smelling trash receptacle is a must. Clean all trash receptacles with a solution of water and bleach inside and outside after removing receptacle liners. This will keep all receptacles smelling fresh and odor-free. In a sickroom, place a thirty-three-gallon trash receptacle, or one of a smaller size, with a lid. The size of the receptacle in the room of the person for whom you provide care will be determined by the need and by the type of care you are providing. When purchasing a laundry basket for dirty laundry, know that the best kind of basket is one that has air ventilation holes without a liner. If a liner is in the laundry basket, the liner must be clean and fresh at all times. If you have a laundry basket without a liner that is well ventilated, you can clean this type of laundry basket with a solution of bleach and water inside and outside. This laundry basket should be utilized only for the person you are caring for. This kind of basket will help to eliminate trapped odors in between washings. Follow the same procedure as above for keeping this basket clean and odor-free.

Plastic Grocery Bags

Save those plastic grocery bags from the market. These bags can be recycled and utilized for kitchen scraps or for waste, such as disposable items from a sickroom. I also place these bags in small wastepaper baskets in all bathrooms. After removing groceries from these bags, I store the bags away until I am ready to utilize them.

Distilled White Vinegar

Distilled white vinegar has many household uses. This product's uses are not limited only to cooking. I've discovered that distilled white vinegar can be used for cleaning, laundering, and deodorizing. This can help you save a lot of money on cleaning products. Most of the ingredients in many of the cleaning products today may be hazardous to one's health. Distilled white vinegar is excellent for use in a sickroom because this product has no adverse side effects.

Distilled White Vinegar for Laundering Colored Clothing

Place half a cup of white distilled vinegar in the wash cycle for laundering colored clothing. This will eliminate body odor, stale odors, and odors from soiled clothing. Rinse all soiled clothing before placing it in the washer.

Distilled White Vinegar and Water

This solution is great. Mix equal parts water and distilled white vinegar in a spray bottle. You can use this solution to clean glass, such as windows. This solution will also eliminate odors from sofas, throw pillows, bed pillows, and mattresses. You can also use it to clean the exhaust hood located over your range. You can also clean your oven's glass door. You can clean the inside of your refrigerator and microwave with this solution. It will eliminate all those bad odors. This solution will also eliminate odor from the air; you will have a little vinegar smell left over, but it will dissipate after five minutes. After that, you will smell nothing but fresh, clean air. For flat-screen television sets and computer monitors, spray solution on a paper towel or cloth and then wipe the screen. Do not spray this solution directly on flat-screen television sets, computer monitors, laptops, or tablets.

Distilled White Vinegar and Baking Soda

This solution will keep your sinks and toilets clog-free and smelling fresh. Place half a cup of distilled white vinegar in your drains or toilet, then add half a cup of baking soda. Allow this mixture to sit for two hours. After letting it sit for two hours, flush your drains with hot water, and then flush your toilet. This will keep your drains clog-free and odor-free. It will keep your toilet fresh and odor-free. This solution will not harm your pipes. I would recommend doing this as least once a month.

Lysol, to Disinfect, Clean, and Deodorize

Lysol is a concentrated disinfectant that kills 99.9 percent of viruses and bacteria. This product can be found in most supermarkets. The size of a standard bottle is twelve ounces. This product is to be diluted with water. One twelve-ounce bottle can last for at least three months depending on how often you utilize this disinfect. I recommend this product for all houses in which a sick person is being cared for. Follow the directions on the bottle for diluting. When diluted with water, Lysol may be utilized for cleaning bathrooms and sickrooms, and wiping down doorknobs and baseboards. You may also add some Lysol to your laundry for either whites or colors. Use a quarter cup of the diluted solution for each load of white or colored laundry. This solution will eliminate odors and disinfect the laundry. Utilize this solution to rinse out soiled clothing before placing the items in the washing machine. Keep a bottle of this solution in all bathrooms and the laundry area.

Clorox Disinfecting Wipes (Clorox Brand Only)

These little wipes are great for keeping your sinks, bathtubs, bathtub wall tile, toilet seats, toilet lids, the outside of the toilet, door handles, and wastepaper baskets fresh-smelling and clean. If your bathroom floor is small enough, you can utilize these wipes to clean your bathroom floor as well. Clorox wipes will clean and eliminate bad odors and germs. These wipes kill 99.9 percent of viruses and bacteria, killing cold and flu viruses, staph, *E. coli*, salmonella, and strep. These wipes are also great for sickrooms with hard surfaces. Remember, the keyword is *Clorox*.

Clorox and Water

A mixture of nine parts water and one part Clorox bleach in a plastic spray bottle is excellent for use in the kitchen. This solution is very good for wiping down countertops and the exterior of the refrigerator. Spray some of this solution in your dishwater to kill germs when washing dishes. This solution will also keep your dishcloths clean and smelling fresh. To remove stubborn stains from your dishcloths, place water (hot or cold) in a bowl, along with one cap of bleach, and soak your dishcloths for an hour. Your dishcloths will come out clean and smelling fresh. Use this solution only for white dishcloths.

Planning Meals and Food Shopping

Meal Planning

In this day and age, it is essential to watch when, how, and where we spend our dollars. The cost of food is going up every day. This is why it's very important to have a grocery list when you go food shopping. It's also important to have a list when you go shopping for anything other than food. Doing so will help you not overspend by keeping you from purchasing things you don't need. Having a list will help you to stay focused and on budget. It will force you to seek out weekly flyers from supermarkets, especially when you purchase the same items on a regular basis. When you utilize flyers from supermarkets, it will help you to plan your menu. I shop at several supermarkets, looking for the best-quality merchandise and the best bang for my buck. Meal planning is essential for the person you are caring for, as well as for yourself. Check with all the physicians of the person for whom you provide care regarding any special diet he or she may require before planning a menu.

If a special diet is necessary, plan your menu around this diet. If a special diet is not recommended, proceed with coming up with a menu of foods that both of you will enjoy. Make a list of the things the person for whom you provide care likes. Using a menu saves you both money and time. Begin by planning your first menu for a ten-day period. Out of these ten days, count on having leftovers for five of them. Then plan a menu for the next ten days. Out of these ten days, plan for another five days' worth of leftovers. Plan for the next ten days as well, utilizing the menu to provide for another five days of leftovers. If you follow this process, it will provide you with thirty days of meals. As you become more comfortable with menus and meal planning, you will begin to add new food items to your menu.

Make Friday a special day. Go for takeout. I find this helps make the person who is being cared for feel special. It also gives you, the caregiver, a break from the kitchen. If the person for whom you provide care is your spouse, then make Friday a date night. He or she will look forward to this treat every week. It will be an added bonus if you select a favorite movie to watch as a couple on your date night. Let everyone know this is your special night. Don't accept phone calls or texts while you're having date night.

Groceries

Keep a pad and pen in the kitchen at all times. When you run out of an item, write it down on your shopping list. Grocery shopping once a week is the best way to go. Read the sell-by dates on all food containers. Remove dry goods from their packages, and place these items in see-through containers with lids. You can obtain see-through containers from any big-box store. This will help you to keep track of what you have in your pantry and what needs to be replaced with just a glance. This procedure will also help to keep bugs and insects from gaining access to your nonperishable food items. This method will also help you save money. Before food shopping, obtain flyers from the stores you most frequently shop. This will help you save time and money and will help you to shop wisely.

Purchasing Meats

Look for manager's specials at the supermarkets you frequent. Plan your menu around the manager's specials if you can. This will help make your meal planning simple and easy. Consider shopping the manager's specials twice a month. This will give you a variety of meats to cook and freeze. This is a very cost-effective method that will help you to save both money and time.

When purchasing the manager's specials, make sure you cook these items the same day they are purchased, and then freeze them. These items are sold at a reduced price because they will perish very quickly, even when placed in the refrigerator. Meats that freeze well after cooking include bottom round roast, chicken, ground turkey, turkey parts, ground beef, turkey breast (with breast bone), lamb, and corned beef.

Fish

Fish is a great source of protein and omega-3 fatty acids. Fresh or frozen fish will do. Everyone should eat fish at least twice a week. Make sure you or the person you are caring for has no allergies to fish. Look for great fish recipes online, or go to the library and check out some great cookbooks dedicated to fish and other seafood.

Starches that Freeze Well

The following starches freeze very well: white potatoes, brown rice, white rice, wheat pasta, and white pasta.

Vegetables That Freeze Well after Cooking

The following vegetables freeze well after cooking: broccoli, cauliflower, green beans, kale, carrots, and rutabaga.

Vegetables Best Eaten in Spring and Summer

Yellow summer squash and zucchini are best eaten in these seasons.

Vegetables Best Eaten in Fall and Winter

Rutabaga, butternut squash, acorn squash, and spaghetti squash are best eaten in the cooler and colder months.

Greens for a salad are great anytime of the year.

Cooking Tips

Spices, Herbs, and Cooking Oils

I love to cook with spices and herbs. I make every attempt to purchase fresh spices and herbs when I can. When I purchase dry herbs and spices, I place them in small glass containers that are made for herbs and spices. I find this method keeps them potent. I also purchase herbs in a squeeze-tube container.

Located in the fresh vegetable section of your supermarket, squeeze-tube herbs can be stored in your refrigerator. I also purchase tubes of tomato paste, garlic paste, and anchovy paste. These items can be found on the shelf of any supermarket.

You can build your knowledge of spices and herbs by going online or visiting your nearest library. When you incorporate spices and herbs into our cooking, it enhances the flavor of your meals. This will inspire you to create new dishes of your own. You can obtain information about cooking with spices, herbs, lemon juice, and cooking oils by going online, watching cooking shows, and visiting your local library. I would recommend the following oils for cooking: olive oil, grape-seed oil, coconut oil, peanut oil, and canola oil. Read the label, go online, and obtain as much information you can on all these items. Experiment with spices, herbs, and lemon juice. The world of spices, herbs, and lemon juice will take you on a journey around the world and back. The only thing you will need for this journey is an open mind and taste buds that crave for more.

Cooking Multiple Meats

Preparing multiple meats is the way to go. You can cook at least three different types of meat at the same time. Following is just an example:

For a bottom round roast (for which you will need a cast-iron Dutch oven), cook it in the oven. You can cook a whole chicken in the oven. Boil corned beef on the range top. After these meats have cooked, allow them to rest for at least thirty minutes before cutting into them. This will allow the juices to redistribute back into the meats. If you don't wait for this process to take place, then when you cut or slice the meat prematurely, all the juices from the meat will be left on the cutting board or platter. This premature cutting will leave your meat dry and tasteless. The foregoing are just examples of how to utilize your time when preparing multiple meats/fowl. Refer to cookbooks, cooking shows, or your library to find recipes that will help you in the cooking of different types of meats/fowl.

Freezing Cooked Meats

After the meats have rested, cut them into portion sizes and place these in quart-size freezer bags. Two portions per freezer bag are enough for one meal for two people. Follow this formula for all cooked meats. Label and date all freezer bags. This will ensure that each portion of meat is eaten by the date on the package. It will also help you keep track of what is in your freezer and how long it's been there.

Do not overpack your freezer. If you overstuff your freezer, the items within will not freeze because you will have created a situation that does not allow the cold air to circulate within your freezer. Remember, your freezer is for storing food to be consumed within a reasonable amount of time, no more than three weeks from the date on the label.

Cooking Fresh and Frozen Vegetables

There are two ways you can cook vegetables: boil them or roast them.

When boiling vegetables, whether fresh or frozen, bring the water to a boil and add a little salt to it. Then add the fresh or frozen vegetables. Boiling frozen vegetables should take five minutes over medium heat. Make sure the person you are caring for is not on a water consumption restriction, as boiled vegetables already have some added water. Roasting fresh or frozen vegetables may be the best way to go. When frozen vegetables are roasted, they retain less water and more of their natural flavor and color.

To roast fresh vegetables, place them on a lined cookie sheet, season with some good spices, and roast in the oven. Frozen vegetables should take about ten minutes at three hundred degrees Fahrenheit. Fresh vegetables may take a little longer at three hundred degrees. Monitor both.

Freezing Cooked Vegetables

After cooking vegetables, allow them to cool. Then place them in a gallon-size freezer bag, which you should label with the contents and the date.

Cooked Dishes that Freeze Well

Cooked dishes that freeze well include macaroni and cheese, pasta sauce with or without meatballs, soups, chili, stews, pot pies, beans, scalloped potatoes, au gratin potatoes, shepherd's pie, turkey or beef burgers, Italian turkey breakfast sausage, curry chicken, gumbo, and chicken cacciatore.

Note: I make my own Italian meatballs, pasta sauce, and Italian turkey breakfast sausage. Try the dishes mentioned in the previous paragraph. You can find recipes for these dishes online at the Food Network or in recipe books. Experiment to make new dishes of your own, remember when it comes to cooking, there is no limit.

Fruits

It is very beneficial to eat fruits that are in season. The following fruits are best eaten in the spring and summer months: berries, pineapples, peaches, plums, cantaloupe, honeydew, grapes, and watermelon.

The following fruits are best eaten in the fall and winter months: apples, pears, oranges, and tangerines.

Bananas can be eaten year-round. Purchase local fruits and vegetables when you can.

Dried fruits are wonderful to eat and are easier to transport than fresh fruits. Good dried fruits are raisins, plums, apricots, and figs. When unable to obtain fresh fruit, dried fruits are the way to go. All fruits, fresh or dried, have great health benefits.

Baking

When it comes to baking, I must say I am limited. I don't do very well with measurements. However, I will share some sweets that I have been successful with, such as zucchini bread and carrot cake. Well, that's it for my baking. I will continue to work on my baking skills. You can find recipes for zucchini bread and carrot cake online at the Food Network or in a recipe book. Your local library will have a vast collection of books on the subjects of cooking, baking, and using spices.

I would like to recommend one more thing. I discovered a wonderful doctor in 1996, while living in Philadelphia. The information I learned from him changed my life. I had begun watching PBS for the cooking programs, which is where

I discovered Dr. Andrew Weil. I got hooked. The information he was sharing got my attention. The information was about *fresh garlic*—yes, garlic—and the many benefits it provides. I got hooked listening to this amazing information.

Dr. Andrew Weil, the author of ten books, attended Harvard, earning a BA degree in biology and an MD from Harvard Medical School. He also studied Chinese medicine for two years in China. He is the author of a wonderful and very informative newsletter. You can go online to obtain more information about Dr. Andrew Weil. The information I received has been lifesaving. I have learned so many wonderful things just from listening to Dr. Weil and reading his newsletters.

Conclusion

Going forward, my wish is to share my experience as a caregiver. I want *How to Become the Best Caregiver* to reach as many caregivers as it does noncaregivers. I want everyone to read *How to Become the Best Caregiver* so they can become the best caregivers they can be. I also want caregivers to learn how take care of themselves amid the daily job of being a caregiver. Thank you, and enjoy.

ABOUT MY WONDERFUL HUSBAND AND OUR LOVE STORY

This is a true love story. I moved to Savannah, Georgia, in October 1998. This was where I met the man who would become my husband, Mr. Muata B. Atiba. I was looking for a barbershop to keep my short haircut looking good. My former barber in Philadelphia, Pennsylvania, had told me to seek out a barbershop as soon as I arrived in Savannah. I had just left Philadelphia on October 7, 1998, arriving in Savannah on October 8, 1998. On Monday, October 9, 1998, I went in search of a barbershop. One block from where I was living, I found a barbershop. Once I'd walked through the door, the first person I saw was Mr. Atiba. Our eyes locked on each other. I knew he was the one because of the chemistry I felt. According to him, he felt it also. I walked over to a barber and asked him if he could maintain my haircut. He said yes. I made an appointment for two weeks from that day.

Well, after that, Mr. Atiba was in the barbershop every time I had an appointment. He asked if we could see each other outside the barbershop. Our first date took place outside the health food store named Brighter Day, across from a beautiful park. He and I went on three dates. On our third date, Mr. Atiba told me that he wanted a more serious relationship. I said to him, "I am not interested in a romantic interlude, but we can be friends."

Mr. Atiba replied, "Okay."

Well, after that meeting, I had not heard from Mr. Atiba in three days. So I called him and asked him, "Are you okay?"

He replied, "Yes." Then he asked, "You want us to be friends, right?"

I replied, "Yes."

He said, "Well, I have enough damn friends. I am looking for someone to spend the rest of my life with. I was married once and have been in several relationships, and they all have failed. I decided to wait and allow the Creator to send me the person meant for me. When you walked through the door of the barbershop, I knew you were the one. We looked at each other and our eyes locked. That was the moment I knew you were the one. My prayers had been answered."

Of course, after hearing this, I had to backtrack. The rest is history. That was twenty-two years ago. Muata lost his left leg up to the hip in 2004. We got married in 2007. Muata developed renal disease in 2011 and began in-center hemodialysis treatments in January 2011. Hemodialysis entails cleaning the blood of toxins. This procedure requires an access site. This may be a catheter access, a graft access, or a fistula access. I provided home hemodialysis treatments for him from 2013 until his passing on March 17, 2018. Having never dated anyone else, we were inseparable for twenty years.

Mr. Atiba worked as a health care provider. He helped me care for my mother and my brother. Muata was my soul mate, my helpmate, my friend, my lover, my confidant, my rock, and my strength. Not only was he my husband but he was also my biggest champion. I have my moments of missing him, and I will continue to have moments of missing him. He encouraged me to write *How to Become the Best Caregiver*. Muata was my biggest supporter. I will always love him. Rest in peace, my love.